A Picture Book for Kids A

Fascinating Facts for Kids About Crabs

All rights reserved. No part of this publication may be reproduced, distributed, or transmitted in any form or by any means, including photocopying, recording, or other electronic or mechanical methods, without the prior written permission of the publisher, except in the case of brief quotations embodied in critical reviews and certain other noncommercial uses permitted by copyright law.

Title: A Picture Book for Kids About Crabs
Series: Fascinating Animal Facts

Cover design: LongTale Books

Published by: LongTale Books
Arlington, VA
http://longtalebooks.com

For information regarding permissions, please contact:
http://longtalebooks.com/contact

First Edition: 2023

Follow our story and art on instagram at https://www.instagram.com/longtalebooksco/

Connect with us on Twitter at https://twitter.com/longtalebooksco

Dedication

For the tireless sense of wonder harbored in every child who is drawn to the miraculous puzzles of nature, this book is for you. To those young minds who watch crabs scuttle across sandy beaches with awe and curiosity, or dream of secrets hidden under the waves - your enthusiasm has inspired every page of this story. This journey into Cara's world seeks not only to entertain, but also nurture that innate love for animal life and fascination for our enchanting marine friends, especially crabs. As we dive together into the wonders beneath our oceans' surface, remember that understanding our natural world is a lifelong adventure—one as captivating and complex as a crab's sideways dance. Happy exploring!

Introduction

Welcome to "A Picture Book for Kids About Crabs," a delightful journey into the world of crabs narrated by our friendly guide, Cara the Crab!

The information presented in this book is vital because it fosters a love and respect for marine life at an early age. Understanding creatures like crabs contributes to a broader comprehension of ecosystems and conservation's importance. It's tailor-made for your little explorers, teaching them fascinating facts about these extraordinary decapods in an engaging and enjoyable way.

So dive in with Cara, uncover ten captivating truths about crabs that will leave you adoring their uniqueness: from their various sizes, appetizing diet, characteristic sideways walk, to their ability to change shells! By the end of this book, young readers will not only have broadened their knowledge about marine life but will also appreciate the wonders of our natural world even more. Remember, every sea creature adds its own spark to Earth's stunning tapestry!

Cara the Crab waves with her claws, eyes gleaming bright. Hello little ones, I'm Cara, that's right! I'm a crab, and it's time to explore, ten fun facts about me, you're sure to adore!

Crabs come in all sizes and shades: From tiny pebble crabs to giant coconut crabs, in colors of the ocean's waves.

We're known as decapods; it sounds like a code. It simply means we have ten legs when on the road!

We crabs live all around the world wide, From the deepest oceans to the seashore's tide.

Crabs love to eat plants and meat. Tiny plankton makes for a tasty treat!

Crabs are experts at playing hide and seek. We burrow in sand or mud deep, safety we seek!

Our hard shell is our super suit. It protects us from dangers and looks very cute!

Crabs walk sideways, it's our funny dance. Give it a try; you might enjoy the prance!

Did you know we grow new shells? We change outfits; it suits us well!

Some crabs live on land while others live in sea. But wherever we are, happy we'll be!

Cara the Crab snuggles into the sand, Tuckered out from touring her wonderful land. Dream of crabs with their shells so bright, And remember, our world is a beautiful sight!

About the Author

John Cole, an engineer with a knack for storytelling, crafts tales that resonate with both young children and eager readers alike. With his three young children often peeking over his shoulder, John's stories are filled with the enchantments of everyday adventures.

Beyond the pages of his books, John's life brims with inspiration. His backyard chickens - Henrietta, Larry, and Fasty Floss - add a touch of whimsy, while the gentle hum of 16,000 bees in his Washington DC suburban backyard reminds him of nature's wonders. Whether he's camping beneath the stars or exploring the outdoors, John's experiences shape the heartwarming narratives he shares.

With a passion for making the world a more magical place, one story at a time, John Cole invites you to dive into his world and discover the wonders that await.

For more tales and adventures, visit https://longtalebooks.com

A Free Book

Reading is the most powerful gift you can give your children, and it should be free. We're giving away free books to any parents and educators when they sign up for our newsletter.

We want to make the gift of reading accessible to all parents and children alike. Get a free book from LongTale Books by signing up to be notified of new releases. We're giving away a free book to everyone who signs up for our newsletter.

Signup now and give the gift of reading for free.

https://longtalebooks.com/free

Made in the USA
Coppell, TX
12 November 2023

24151269R00017